The Conscious Hustle

Business as a path to wealth & awakening

By Dane Tomas

First published in 2015 by Dane Tomas Enterprises Pty Ltd
Melbourne, Australia

© Dane Tomas Enterprises Pty Ltd
The moral rights of the author have been asserted.

National Library of Australia Cataloguing-in-Publication data:

Author:
     Tomas, Dane
Title:
     The Conscious Hustle / Dane Tomas
ISBN:
     978-1508725404
Subjects:
     Business
     Entrepreneurship
     Psychology
     Spirituality

Editor-in-chief: Maria Martello
Cover Design: Vanessa Maynard

This book is a SpiritCast Network Book
www.SpiritCastNetwork.com.au

For my grandparents.

"Millionaires don't use astrology.
Billionaires do."

— *J. P. Morgan*

A CERTAIN WAY.

I have found that business, if approached in a certain way is a powerful vehicle for accelerating our development as a human beings as well as being a very effective method for delivering transformation and growth to large groups of people.

This book is an introduction to that "certain way" of doing things that converts a business from just being a way of making a living into a transformative pathway.

I also believe that entrepreneurs, more than any other group, are equipped with the right mindset and skills to genuinely change the way we do things on this planet for the better.

This book is for anyone who wants to forge a new path using business as a vehicle to improve the world we live in and live a freer, more exceptional life.

It's for spiritual types who are wanting to develop their business as well as business people who know that aligning their business with their higher purpose is the only way to really take it to the next level.

And… if you're already in both categories – let's be friends!

WHAT'S CONSCIOUSNESS GOT TO DO WITH IT?

I realised as I was writing this that the conscious hustle sounds some type of bizarre dance — and in a way it is.

It's a journey on which we learn to manage the interplay of two seemingly separate paths; the path of business success and the path of personal awakening.

There is a dogma on this planet that portrays the idea that the spiritual and the material are somehow separate. From the idea of physical desire as sinful, to the idea that money is the root of all evil – I believe this myth of separation is the cause of a great deal of harm and suffering.

People have been trained over generations that money, wealth and influence are best left to religious and state authority figures and that individuals have no real power.

Humans have also been taught that they are not connected to the divine and that some sort of intermediary is required in order to commune with higher powers.

Although I think these beliefs are dissolving in many arenas I still come across a lot of resistance and emotional responses in people when I suggest that EVERYTHING in life can be a spiritual practice and that the areas of wealth creation and business building are no exception to this rule.

BEING V DOING.

The world seems to be divided into people who are good at "being" and people that are good at "doing" with only a small handful of open hearted, consciously connected people who can actually kick arse and get things done.

It is my intention to help connect the spiritual and the material, the being and the doing and the yin and the yang aspects of us together; in order to build a tribe of sustainable, purpose aligned, socially conscious entrepreneurs who can genuinely influence the direction of this planet's evolution.

POVERTY CONSCIOUSNESS DISCLAIMER:

If you are strongly attached to the idea that rich people are bad and poor people are good and that the only way forwards is for us to dismantle the economic system and radically shrink our desires — this book is not going to be an agreeable read for you. (Even though we probably agree on a lot of the outcomes and things that need to happen for life on earth to continue, I'm don't, at this stage see political revolution (at least not by itself) as the way to make it happen.

I believe that since business is currently the dominant paradigm on the planet, business people need to connect to their spirituality and that spiritual people need to get good at business. I love helping both of these things happen.

This book seeks to go beyond conditioned responses and re-write what's possible in the area of business and introduce the idea that we can use it as a spiritual path and that it is ok to be rich too — although we may need to redefine how we measure that!

CHAPTER ONE

SURVIVE OR THRIVE

"Spirit without matter is motionless. Matter without spirit is expressionless"

— *Dr John Demartini*

THE TIPPING POINT:

In 2005 I sat in a random London pub with my best friend.

We were both completely broke, literally pooling our entire net worth just for a couple of pints of beer, unsure of how we we're going to get through the next few days and we were feeling quite low.

" I don't wanna go" he said.

"No neither do I. Ok fuck it… give me your phone."

I called the hospitality company we were begrudgingly working for and told them we wouldn't be attending that night's job.

The woman who had hired us was understandably pissed at this last minute cancellation but we both felt strangely empowered by the situation. That night would turn out to be one of the funnest adventures I've had in my life.

We'd been in London for a year and it had been a dark, depressing year at that. Everything I'd tried to achieve seemed to have failed and constantly not having enough to make ends meet wasn't helping. The more I reflected on it, the more I realised that my ideas about money were naïve and that I actually wanted to be financially successful.

"Fuck this dude. I wanna do something I love doing."

"Yeah me too. Let's go home and get rich."

Something re-set itself inside me at that moment. Like so many people who make a change in their lives I'd hit a point of no-return that FORCED me to re-evaluate.

Up until then I'd been of the opinion that being financially abundant was only for 'old people' and 'wankers'. Something began to shift once I got really clear on what I wanted – I wanted to do something I loved, make money doing it... and, I realised, almost as an afterthought – I really, really wanted to help people too.

I wanted to do something that would both leave my mark on the world and have a positive impact on a large number of human beings. I felt absolutely certain I could do it. I just didn't know how yet.

The key point of this book is simply to point towards what might be possible.

To start people asking better questions and realising that it doesn't have to be an either/or reality.

There is ALWAYS a way to have BOTH.

It's just that usually being able to see that requires a big change of our point of view.

We don't need a revolution. We need to evolve.

When amphibians evolved into land-dwelling creatures they didn't do it by killing all the fish. They simply became (very slowly) something that was far beyond a fish.

I think we can become something far beyond employee-consumer drones.

LIZARD PEOPLE RUN THE WORLD.

Can I eat it? Can I fuck it? Is it a threat? Should I freeze? Should I run?

The ancient, reptilian part of our brain that sits underneath everything else is REALLY good at keeping us alive.

The brain stem (hereby referred to scientifically as the lizard brain) "cares" only about survival, territory and pro-creation. If we are alive and well and everything seems (from a survival point of view) to be working, it will do everything it can to keep things THE SAME.

Too bad if you want to double your income, lose some weight or do anything else that requires radically changing your world view, your identity and your routine.

Our oldest circuitry really isn't designed for us to thrive. The amygdala (aka lizard brain) is concerned with only survival and a lot of our emotional responses to life seem to be set up the same way too. We are wired mostly to move toward pleasure and away from pain. Too bad if we've associated pain to what we consciously want and pleasure to what we don't. The lizard brain will kick in anytime we get too close to an outcome that seems like it might be a threat to our survival.

This isn't done through slow consideration but through knee jerk reactions like throwing yourself out of the path of an oncoming vehicle (or a wooly mammoth), but and also from underhanded tactics that can range from subtle sabotage (like never responding to that email) to panic attacks and discomfort when we pursue a new direction in life.

Almost everything you need to do, think and feel in order to be abundantly wealthy is the direct opposite of how the lizard brain thinks.

To be wealthy we need to think long term and often to delay gratification.

The lizard brain only cares about us being safe and well fed right now.

To build a company we need to take risks, let go of control and do other things that the lizard brain considers a total no-no.

Since we live in a world with actually very few genuine threats to our survival, but many thousands of opportunities to do things that could trigger our most primal selves concerns about survival, we pretty much live in a state of continual dissonance with our amygdala.

This can go into overdrive the day you walk out of your day job and don't know where the next paycheque (i.e., food source) is coming from.

HAVE YOUR CAKE AND EAT IT!

So even "normal" business requires going against our deep-seated survival programming. What about if we not only want to be financially successful but want to build a business that really aligned with who we are at the highest level, a "conscious" business. It's an even bigger ask which means we're gonna have to overcome an even larger amount of our survival programming.

This is why most people never escape the nine to five. It's just too scary. Essentially the boss substitutes in for Mummy or Daddy and we get to relax because we know that in exchange for our loyalty, hard work and acceptance of drudgery our basic survival needs will be met week in and week out.

We also get the soothing feeling of "fitting in" and being part of a tribe of "normal" people. Maybe not joyous, world-changing, purpose-aligned, deeply fulfilled people but at least we get to belong. More on this later.

We become enslaved by our attachment to stability and certainty. On the surface we've entered into a "time for money" agreement with our employer but what's happened in many cases is we're auctioning off something much more real – our life force!

My intention isn't to mock anyone working a job. Except for the Gen-Y "natural" entrepreneurs I sometimes meet who've never had a job, most of us have been there and most people working for someone else have plenty of valid reasons for doing so. The important part is to separate what's "real" (I have to feed my children) from what's psychological (I need to feel secure/hopefully now my parents will respect me).

The first stage of the conscious entrepreneurial journey is helping our frontal lobe get a clear separation between our real and actual needs, and our strong emotional attachments to ideas such as security and certainty.

I've taken a lot of "risks" in my entrepreneurial journey and the question I always ask myself is:

"Could I possibly die if this goes wrong?"

Strangely enough the answer has always been "No".

As a second fail safe I like to imagine the worst case scenario (life coaches look away now) and spend a few minutes outlining how I would manage the situation if everything did indeed fall to pieces.

With that handled I find my survival brain can relax and I can get on with focusing on building and creating.

KILL THE EMPLOYEE IN YOU.

You've probably worked out by now that this book isn't targeted at people who choose to value security over freedom.

On top of the lizard brain survival stuff (which is hard to permanently get rid of but I have developed a process for clearing it if you want to accelerate your journey) we also have a lot of 'employee' conditioning.

The current educational model is primarily designed to churn out employees.

It teaches us that making mistakes is to be avoided, that rules are to be followed without question, that security is attainable and that we "deserve" an hourly rate, sick pay and holidays. This process generally does its level best to train young humans to be conformists (and by default) consumers.

Again the exact opposite of the beliefs and attitudes you might need to go out and create your own company.

It's not surprising that a lot of successful entrepreneurs are high school and university drop outs. It can get hard to juggle to contradictory mindsets.

Even if you're a long term entrepreneur it's likely that there are little bits of employee programming still hiding away in the back of your noggin that sometimes affect your planning or make you aim too small or play "too safe".

Perhaps the most destructive implication of being an employee is the idea of being "owed something". I worked therefore I get sick pay. I worked for 30 years so now I get a pension.

There is a cause and effect assumption that our wellbeing and rewards are in the hands of someone else and there is also an addiction to the idea of "fairness". Being taken care of by someone else is also quite addictive!

I find that entrepreneurs don't harbor this childish obsession with what's "fair" quite as strongly as people who work for a large companies and who don't have a stake in the success of that company.

Psychologically the employee is still in a sort of financial child stage of development. There is an assumption that "I should be rewarded just for turning up" and a total disconnection from the reality that it is the results that we create that determine what we receive.

There is also an embedded assumption, which deepens the longer we spend in the role of an employee — that "going out on my own" or "surviving off my own talent" is impossible or at least difficult and frightening.

To become an entrepreneur is to walk off into the woods by yourself – to leave the safe confines of the village and to trust that everything will be ok, even if a wolf does eat you.

I see the whole entrepreneurial pathway as a never-ending heroes journey.

The entrepreneur develops a more mature understanding of cause and effect.

I don't get paid "because I deserve it". I get paid because I found a way to create value for someone else, in a way that they wanted and to charge them for it.

If I'm to survive alone in the forest I need to learn how to hunt or forage and to build shelter. Maybe overtime I'll grow a garden. You get the idea I'm sure.

As an entrepreneur we become more in tune with reality. We begin to treat the world and our business as a feedback system that teaches us whether we're on the right track or not.

We try something, it either works or it doesn't, we take the feedback and we adjust our behaviour. There is a direct feedback between whether our ideas work and whether we eat. The basis for becoming an entrepreneur (conscious or otherwise) is to cultivate trust in yourself at a base level.

We realise that we can go anywhere we want, do anything and that we really are in charge of our life direction. The attitude must be:

NO MATTER WHAT HAPPENS –
I KNOW I'LL BE FINE.

YOU'RE CARRYING GRANDMOTHER'S BAGGAGE.

On top of everything I've mentioned so far, we also have received centuries (even millennia) of emotional conditioning. This affects everything from our sex life to our perceptions about money to our physical health and wellbeing.

You know those habits you have that you've tried to change but can't?

Some of those came from your parents, no big surprise there; what pop psychology doesn't teach us though, is that our conditioning is handed down generation to generation.

The line between "nature and nurture" blurs greatly once we realise that emotional patterns are passed down the ancestral line just like genes and can be responsible for many of the same things we've learned to blame on our genes.

Depending on your ancestry you may be running patterns that began with one of your ancestors in Genghis khans' time.

I've cleared money blocks for a French friend of mine that dated back to the French revolution. It's quite easy to understand how being alive in that tumultuous time could cause you to attach terror to the idea of "being rich".

In my case my family comes from the north of England, my roots go right back through where the industrial revolution began and BOTH sets of my grandparents worked in the cotton mills for most of their lives.

That gives you some insight into why I decided to invent processes for clearing emotional baggage and why specifically I felt the need to clear blockages around financial wealth, worth and scarcity!

Back in those days an entrepreneur was someone who could afford a factory or two. The reason I know so much about this stuff is I've been pushing against, clearing up, chipping away at, and eventually dynamiting holes in my cultural programming since early 2000.

I've used and abused psychedelics, kinesiology, NLP, EFT, meditation practice, tantric yoga and every personal development and wealth mindset practice I could get my hands on to "re-format my hard drive" and align myself with the sort of freedom of choice and behavioural flexibility that I believe should be available to everyone.

THIS IS NOT A CONSPIRACY BOOK:

I'm writing this book from a place of :

"We create our reality and can have pretty much whatever we want".

However, much like the matrix — it IS essential we wake up first.

Less than 0.0001% of the people on this planet have wealthy ancestors.

That means if we genuinely intend to create a reality of abundance for ourselves we have to break the chains that connect us to the past and learn how to think and act in ways that our grandparents and parents were not able to teach us.

From the point of view of being a "conscious creator" the cultural narratives we live inside of set us up in a way that is completely wrong.

Politicians often campaign on a platform of "more jobs" and large amounts of racism and xenophobia is based around the scarcity myth that comes with this:
e.g. "they took our jobs" and "there isn't enough to go around".

Most people buy into this because they don't see that MOST jobs are a form of modern slavery. (If you're getting paid well to either learn a skill you need or do what you love on your own terms then that's an exception to this statement.) Most people I speak to are not in that situation.

So rare is the individual who thinks: "Fuck having a job – I want to be me".

Rarer still is the person who decides "I'm going to be a multimillionaire, whilst doing what I love, whilst living in alignment with my highest purpose of serving others and whilst minimising my negative impact on the planet."

This is what I decided I wanted in 2012. It was a much deeper, more explicit re-stating of the promise I'd made to myself back in 2005.

It took a huge amount of emotional work and personal development before I could even consider that as a realistic possibility.

Now, I'm not yet a millionaire, and I still have a lot to learn about money and business but within two years of making that decision I was earning my old yearly wage every month and I was doing it by helping people clear up their emotional blocks.

When I realised this had happened I knew the main reason was because I'd changed what I believe to be possible and changed my level of vibration to match those beliefs.

MONKEY SEE MONKEY DO:

At our current level of evolution we are still most accurately described as "social primates."

We decide what "normal" is by looking around at the people we know and comparing ourselves to what they are doing. We also decide our "worth" by comparing ourselves to others.

This can get very confusing when we have many social circles and are bombarded with images of the wealthy, famous and powerful on a daily basis.

We are also very susceptible to the opinions of the people around us. It's amazing how liberally people who know nothing about the path you are on will dispense intentionally well-meaning-but-useless advice.

Taking advice about your business from someone who has only every been an employee is like taking fitness training tips from a fat man. It is foolish to take guidance from someone who knows nothing of the path you are embarking on.

In addition to this, the tribal structure slows down our growth as long as we fear losing its support and warmth. People unconsciously can begin to act very strangely if you start working on raising your financial worth or your level of consciousness as it begins to reflect their own inadequacies back to them. The same thing happens at each new level of influence and responsibility.

If everyone you know makes $150K a year running their own micro-business or functioning as a sole-trader things can get weird when you announce you want to make $2M a year whilst hanging out at the beach.

CHAPTER ONE EXERCISES:

STEP ONE:
Write down any goal or idea that you have been procrastinating because it seems to big and scary or risky:

STEP TWO:
Write down the worst-case scenario that could realistically happen if you go for it:

STEP THREE:
Write down how you would handle the worst-case scenario to minimise its negative impact:

CHAPTER TWO

TRIBES

No problem can be solved from the same level of consciousness that created it

– Albert Einstein

PERCEPTION IS PROJECTION:

"I sat there at the back of the classroom, black hoody and baggy jeans on, all my frowns and hip-hop swagger masking the fact that I was getting extremely triggered by all the talk of money, and business and success whilst "serving from the heart.""

These people were "fake wankers" and were "full of shit" I told myself, and I decided I was in the wrong place.

When they mentioned "making $25,000 a month" I almost threw up.

I was face-to-face with what I would later describe as my "poverty conditioning" and in truth – I was scared.

This was in 2008 and I was at the intake weekend for a life-coaching training that'd I'd forked out my hard-earned money for from rap gigs and telemarketing, for and now I was finally in the room and I felt out of my depth.

Amongst all the fears that were hiding beneath the surface was the one that said: "If I hang out in these sort of environments with these sorts of people I'll change and I won't be able to hang out with my cool (but very broke) rapper friends that smoke weed and get drunk".

I was right. Things would never be the same again. I'd lose some friends, make some new ones and temporarily depart from a few who I'd meet around the next bend.

I learned that who you surround yourself with, and what those people talk about really does shape your life's trajectory.

CONSENSUS REALITY.

If it's our lizard brain that's running our survival behaviours then it's the monkey brain (not scientific terms) that takes charge of everything to do with social hierarchy, belonging to the group and determining our status.

Our society mostly functions at this level.

Anyone who's studied the dark arts of influence and persuasion at all quickly starts to realise that most of our decisions are not made logically but emotionally and that most of those emotions are geared to get us to follow authority, do what the group does, and make sure we fit in and belong to one tribe or another.

In the 1950s when modern advertising was born, advertisers began using all of these newly (discovered?) psychological principles to motivate people to buy more. The idea of consumerism began to take hold.

We began buying things because they made us sexier, because they promised us confidence, because authority figures and high status individuals endorsed them and perhaps, worst of all — we began to buy things because we didn't want to feel left out.

The concept that buying things could not only meet a basic need but could be a form of expression, a pathway to fulfilment and a way to increase positive qualities (like confidence or sex appeal) took root.

Don't get me wrong – I AM a consumer.

I do my best to be conscious about it and have learnt that too much "stuff" slows me down and wastes my time and energy but I'm still sitting here with my MacBook, iPhone and iPad all next to each other.

There is no question in my mind that the intensity of media and marketing brainwash has created a dependent, docile herd from a large section of the human race.

Using TV shows, movies and massive sporting events, humans are able to project our need to overcome adversity and experience growth onto external mediums to make up for the fact that we don't experience it in our jobs and careers.

How else could we withstand the drudgery of waking up each morning to work for someone else's agenda that isn't aligned with our own in order to pay our rent and our bills and if we're lucky — to party on the weekend and maybe even tuck a little bit away for a rainy day?

Sorry. Did that sound cynical?

I'm neither anti consumer nor anti capitalist — but — the only way we can evolve past our current level of existence is to raise the consciousness and discernment with which we engage in these (or any other) isms.

This tribal level of engagement exists in all environments where we get more than 2 individuals connected together and we are far more bound by the rules of the tribe than we can ever recognise.

It starts with our family dynamic and expanding into various social groupings we evolve numerous sets of rules for governing status and belonging.

The single biggest fear on the "monkey level" is rejection.

This (mostly unconscious) need to belong locks our society at a certain level of consciousness. "Normal" people work jobs, buy things on credit, are content to work for others and don't ask a lot of big questions like:

"What's the point of it all?" and "What's my actual purpose?"

Those questions get people a bit edgy because they might lead to unusual methods of enquiry and definitively non-consumer behaviour, non-herd behaviour.

Ask any seasoned tripper and they'll tell you why psychedelics are illegal:

"Because they open your mind man and make you realise this whole thing isn't real"

Uh oh. We're in edgy territory here.

Of course, Buddhism does the same thing but it takes rather a lot of meditation practice before you start having a direct experience of the illusory nature of consensus reality.

We also learn from what's around us. Our expectations and the realms of possibility are governed mostly by what we have seen and what we are told.

Once again I don't think exactly that we are programmed strategically by a coherent structure of ruling elites, rather, I think that we've evolved to follow the pack, learned to not ask for anything too far outside of the status quo and have learned to basically settle for what we're given by circumstances.

I also think that the "big" monkeys have risen to the top and get to decide how the bananas are distributed. You get the idea.

This is where the problem of "lets just redistribute all the wealth" lies. People have been conditioned to believe what they are worth — each of us carries a certain "wealth resonance" with us. An energetic blueprint that tells us what we are worth and how big of a game we can play. Unless we consciously work on stretching that blueprint we will stay at the same relative same level of wealth and influence as our parents.

This is the hidden reason why the children of the wealthy tend to remain wealthy and peasant's children have to work very hard to become anything other than a peasant. We are each conditioned for our position.

If everyone were attuned to the reality that abundance were their birthright, if we realised on a deep core level that there were no real limits to what we could be, do or experience it really would be difficult to maintain any sort of class system.

Unfortunately that's not how it works. Our parents' beliefs and emotions around wealth, worth, business and what's possible inform our own from an early age.

Furthermore the majority of our family and friends will reinforce these expectations and conditions of belonging.

Things get very problematic when we decide to "do our own thing". The emotional clearing process I take people through called 'The Spiral' clears up the emotional blocks that prevent people from being themselves. The first ones we clear are 'shame' and 'guilt'. It's amazing how many people start doing "what they always wanted" once the patterns of shame and guilt have been dropped from their lives.

So we've learned that we're primarily set up to focus on survival and moving away from negative feelings — even when we have all the resources we need at our finger tips.

The better we get at designing the life and business we want to have, the easier it is to create that. There's just one thing that can possibly get in our way: other people.

For those of you earlier on the path, this chapter is sort of a friendly "heads up". For those of you who've been doing your thing for a while this will be more of a confirmation of something you've already experienced.

The people we surround ourselves with have a huge impact on what we are capable of.

Like attracts like right? We connect with and spend time with people who are "like" us in some way.

They either came from the same place, have the same interests, work at the same job, are part of the same culture and most binding of all, are part of the same family.

"YOU'VE CHANGED MAN"

So what happens if you start to change?

What happens if your vision begins to expand, your values (at least your conditioner, surface level values) begin to shift and you begin to start thinking and behaving differently?

This is one of the ways in which the entrepreneurial and the spiritual path have a lot in common. Once we start on one of them — we are going to lose some friends.

On the upside we are going to bring some of our friends along with us and we are going to meet ALL kinds of interesting people on the way too.

Often when I share one of the old personal development clichés "look at the top 5 people you spend your time with — this is who you will become" people can get a bit triggered. "So you're saying I should just ditch my friends because they don't make any money?" they might say.

That's not exactly my message and I'd like to go into it in a little more detail here.

The idea of resonance tells us that similar ideas, emotions, places, concepts, behaviours and people all vibrate at similar levels.

When we start opening our minds to new realms, many of the people in our world won't be receptive to our discoveries on the other side.

As we start to change our behaviours and our standards other people have to re-calibrate how they see us and interact with us. They also have to deal with seeing their own reflection in our achievements.

If we suddenly start promoting ourselves, start making increased amounts of money and start experiencing success — it's going to push buttons for SOME of the people around us.

The more this continues, the more our new resonance continues to come in, the further we travel the more it will hit a make or break point — the people in our lives will have to either deal with whatever issues our success brings up for them or they will have to depart from our lives.

Of course there are those people who will love and support us regardless of what we believe, or what we achieve — but the fact remains it will become increasingly painful for us, and anyone around us who doesn't really 'fit' with our new vibration.

The other, more proactive side of this is that we can rapidly accelerate our growth by seeking out other people on a similar path.

Ideally this will take the form of friends who are living by similar principles as us as well as finding mentors who are further along down the path we want to travel.

Don't underestimate the power of this. People who isolate themselves are doomed to struggle against the consensus reality which is:

Believe what you're told. Accept what your offered. Fit in. Work a job. Etc.

For those of you who may be involved in less "mainstream" circles there is a similar process that applies.

In "spiritual" communities there is often a strong "anti-money" "anti-establishment" value system that dominates. Ironically this can demand conformist behaviour of its own.

Those sentiments are not compatible with the path I'm describing because despite being hidden in loving language and smelling like sage — those are still fear-based, lack-based world views.

Anyone who refuses to fully explore the limits of their potential will become very uncomfortable when you start exploring yours.

They may tell you that your ideas won't work, or that you shouldn't charge decent amounts of money for them. I tend to only take advice from people who have proven themselves in a given field. The number of people who are not successful in business but happily dispense advice is staggering.

Seek people who know what they are doing and seek others on a similar compatible path. These two things are essential not just to ensure success but in order to feel belonging and kinship with other people.

You are not alone. There are 1000s of people moving towards what we can describe as conscious entrepreneurship because it is an INEVITABLE step on the ladder of self-actualization (see Maslow's hierarchy of needs & spiral dynamics).

CHAPTER TWO EXERCISES:

Make a list of the 5 people you spend most of your time with:

Make a list of any skills, traits or attributes not currently present in your top 5 friends:

Brainstorm who or what sorts of people you would like to add to your list of friends, mentors and influences:

CHAPTER THREE

POWER

"Raise your energy, people will be pulled to you;
when they show up – bill 'em"

– Stuart Wilde

I sat on the beach, huddled beneath a rocky outcrop trying to light the pipe away from the wind. It was my first time smoking "changa" a natural mixture that combines the psychedelic compound DMT with various other herbs to make it more smoke-able and easier to absorb.

I knew from experience that clarity of intention is what separates a shamanic or divinatory experience from just "tripping balls".

I had marked out a circle of stones beneath the cliff and set my intentions very clearly. I asked: "Show me my purpose. I want to know my purpose".

The mixture was super strong. I took long slow tokes and held it deep in my lungs for as long as I possibly could. On the 3rd toke the outside world began to fade away and I was undeniably in another dimension.

I was in a fractal realm of colourful, jewelled structures pulsating with knowledge and face to face with what resembled a preying mantis (it wasn't exactly that but I think it's what my brain decided to see it as) It was simultaneously male and female; the king and queen of a realm beyond the senses.

We began to communicate with words but soundlessly. The creature 'explained' that it was the keeper of all knowledge and I realised I had the opportunity to ask it questions. There was a low, never-ending chiming sort of note playing in the background and the jewelled structures were endlessly morphing into different shapes.

I asked various questions about my life purpose, about love, sex and human behaviour and received clear, powerful answers to each of them.

Then I asked:

"What about money?"

There was a weird sort of quiet chittering sound. It was laughing.

"You humans and your money. It is pointless. Money is not a cause.

It is an… effect."

"Ok then. What's the cause?"

"Power."

With that last word I felt all the transmissions I'd been receiving. The geometric patterns were affecting my own structure on some level. I was downloading information and I knew it would be a long time before I integrated it all.

The jewelled structures began to fade and so did the creature. I could once again see the beach, the rocks and the ocean although for a while the light structures were interwoven in and through everything I could see.

It gave me the impression that the reality I'd glimpsed was present all the time. An underlying causal framework that was like the architectural blueprint for what we consider "normal" reality.

I was could see I was living in the world of effects. A world where our human brains made things look and feel the way it needed them to in order to make sense of things. Time was bullshit. Space wasn't what we thought. Money was even less real than those two. It seemed evident that what mattered in terms of creating and attracting was 'Power'.

The word had such a dirty ring to it before the experience. Now it felt beautiful. They weren't talking about political power or financial power or social status — they meant the ACTUAL power to create and attract.

From that day forward I began to realise that all humans have power. We've just trained ourselves not to use it.

THE QUANTUM LEVEL:

That psychedelic experience confirmed what I've encountered hundreds of times during deep meditation and what my attempts to understand quantum physics and neuroscience have implied to me.

That reality doesn't really work the way we think it does. The conversation with the praying mantis people (yes I actually wrote that) confirmed something that my wealth building mentors have all emphasised in one set of language or another — money is not a cause — it's an effect.

The average human doesn't understand this. Because our brains are better at dealing with "things" than abstract concepts, people try to treat money as a "thing". It's simply a symbol that we've (sort of) agreed to using as a means to measure value.

What we really crave though are the means to sustain our lives and then the experiences that add meaning and value to our lives. We believe money can give us these so we try to "get money".

The weird insectoid laughter rings in my head whenever I slip into the "get money" mentality.

I have learned that my job is to create things, to birth ideas, to connect existing ideas together in a way that creates value — usually in the forms of growth and evolution for other human beings.

The more I've decided to be a "cause" rather than an "effect" the less I've had to worry about what's in the bank and the less I take life at face value.

Instead I now think of life in terms of face value.

I believe that the visual way we perceive our lives limits and confuses us and prevents us from really tapping into what's going on.

It's as if we're peering through two tiny slits, looking at a multidimensional tapestry of swirling chaos, energy and potential and our conditioned human mind processes it and creates a visual model inside of our heads.

On a surface level our experience is "real" but how real is real?

In the enlightenment the dogma of the church was replaced by the new dogma of science. Anything that cannot be measured, deconstructed or logically explained is now dismissed.

This model has brought tremendous growth and acceleration to the human race — but… it has its limits too.

When our identity dissolves completely (whether through psychedelics, meditation or sexual ecstasy) things lose their substance.

We are able to experience the world beyond the conceptual realm — a realm of swirling energy and potential. This is not something we can yet measure — it has to be understood experientially.

My best understanding of "actuality" (as in what's actually going on outside of our heads as opposed to the reality we make up to make it make sense) is that it's vibrational. All things (whether a rock a table, a person or a thought form) vibrate at a certain level. Some things (like the work of Mozart for example) vibrate at a high level of consciousness — and we can feel this when we listen to it. Other things (such as the emotion of shame for example) vibrate at a very low level of consciousness.

When we are around a person deep in shame energy or we feel it ourselves, we contract, we become drowsy, we have no energy.

In this way we "attract" events and circumstances into our life. When someone is locked in a "victim" cycle it's almost inevitable that another awful thing is going to happen to them. The mental narrative they carry as well as the emotions, the behaviours and the belief systems that are running inside them continue to generate a certain vibration which will continue to attract more of the same.

The book "Power v Force" by Dr. David Hawkins outlines a "scale of consciousness" which provides and awesome understanding of this idea.

If you gain only one learning from this book let it be this:

Success is vibrational. If we want to consistently experience ANYTHING we must raise our vibration to a level that resonates with that experience.

The entire journey of the conscious entrepreneur is one of raising our resonance.

The Wealth Upgrade Sessions I do with entrepreneurs take them through a process that first measures and then raises their "wealth resonance".

Once we begin dropping patterns like shame, guilt, fear, resentment, our wealth resonance rises rapidly. It's amazing what happens after we do this. New people, more money, different circumstances turn up — sometimes very "quickly".

The entire name of the "game" is about raising our own resonance and then through whatever we do — using our abilities to raise the resonance of our tribe and then of the planet.

ALIGNED ACTION:

Initially this process of raising our resonance begins as follows — we decide we want to create something in the world, we begin visualising it and get clear on what it looks like. We begin speaking about it and organising our thoughts and resources — next we must act.

Many people who understand the idea of resonance or attraction take a passive attitude to life — "if it's meant to be it will happen". There's nothing wrong with this attitude in and of itself — indeed the ability to be receptive is critical in the process of creating/manifesting/attracting, but there are two sides to every coin.

Yin/yang, passive/active, feminine/masculine are all creative polarities. In order to make something happen, there must be action. Before and after the action there is time and space for reflection, recovery and re-alignment but everyone I know that is in anyway successful is capable of taking action and of taking action quickly.

The best way to test an idea is to act on it.

In the world of business this means SELLING, MARKETING and DELIVERING.

If I decide that I have an awesome idea for a workshop — the first thing I need to do is to offer it to people — for a price. I don't design the content, book the venue or any of those secondary activities – I float the idea and if it seems like something people want – I start taking credit card numbers and processing deposits.

This launches something into being. I've invested my energy and others have begun to invest theirs.

This is part of the conscious entrepreneurial manifesto.

Take action, observe the results, change your approach if necessary — rinse and repeat.

Too many people seem to think the value or the power is in the idea.

Ideas are very cheap. There are trillions of them floating in the ether. It's the person who brings an idea into the world that creates value for other people and receives rewards and abundance in exchange.

Most people get hung up on sales and marketing. The two most important functions of any business are so loaded with misconceptions and negative associations that people can't see the beauty of these two functions.

My advice on this is simple — don't judge based on how companies you don't like sell and market to you. Recognise that there are brands and individuals you LOVE that you interact with every day — that are selling and marketing to you constantly.

First let's figure out what these words really mean:

To sell, comes from the Icelandic "selje" — which means "to serve". So selling (when it's aligned with the heart) is a form of service. If you offer something that you KNOW benefits the world then obviously you would want as many people as possible to benefit from it right? Great.

Marketing is really the art of knowing WHO you want to serve (sell) and getting your message to them.

The more you care about your ideal client (addressed later) and the clearer your message is, the more effortless, fun and congruent sales and marketing will become for you.

Many people want to wait until everything is perfect before they sell their product or service. This isn't entrepreneur thinking. This is scarcity thinking. You need to accept that nothing will ever be "perfect" and that in fact the best way to test an idea is to sell and deliver it to some people.

You will learn more from the doing and the execution of the idea than you will from 100 years of analysis.

People like to spend money on offices, computers, business cards, pretty branding and even hiring staff — all of these things are far secondary to the primary purpose of business — to sell and deliver your life changing services and products.

I believe this is a sophisticated form of resistance — a way that we can play at business without actually doing THE BUSINESS! There are 2 useful short term metrics that tell us how were doing – 1. Service/products delivered. 2. Money brought in. These are the month-to-month yardsticks of whether we're moving forwards. Whether we're heading in the right direction is another story entirely and can only really be assessed once we've actually moved in a direction!

CHAPTER THREE EXERCISES:

STEP ONE:
Write down a description of your perfect day. Where would you be, what would you be doing, who would you be with, how would you be feeling? Include your business life, love life, environment, health and well being and recreation etc:

STEP TWO:

What 3 simple changes could you make to move your life closer to living your perfect day?

STEP THREE:

Work out the circumstances required as well as the monthly living expenses required to live your perfect day: (this will inform your financial targets in the spiritual business plan).

CHAPTER FOUR

LOVE, MONEY & SYSTEMS

"I'm not a businessman, I'm a business. man"

– Jay Z

I built my emotional clearing process "The Spiral" by cross referencing the chakra system, with the scale of consciousness, with spiral dynamics and clearing the emotions that occurred at each level with a process I invented called a "root clear".

I'm kind of a nerd like that.

When it came to taking myself through level 4 – I really didn't know what was going to happen. In the chakras the 4th one is the heart chakra — in spiral dynamics it's the "blue" meme, which is really about large-scale organisation and often carries a moralistic feel. It's also where complex systems start to arrive in the picture of human development.

I just didn't understand how love and organisation were interlinked; it didn't make any sense to me, at least not until AFTER I'd done the clearing.

As we began removing the blocks around my relationship to "love" I started getting visions of my birth flashing through my eyes — complete with 1970s fashion and the feelings of what it must've been like for my parents having their first child. There was also something else emerging from the memory.

I'd always tried to keep the idea of "the soul" out of my work and focus more on the psycho-emotional aspects of it but after this particular initiation all of that would change.

As we cleared the blocks around "Love" I had a crystal clear memory of my birth or at least the moments just after my birth. I could remember my "attitude" as I turned up on planet earth.

I was fully conscious and intelligent and I was fucking pissed off!

No one had told me how dense it was going to be, how low the vibrations were going to be. No one had explained to me that I would be weak and powerless and no one had explained that I would be bound to a certain set of individuals by physical dependency and emotional attachment.

My very first thoughts we're "This isn't fair" and "I hate this place". After that something happened and I lost touch with this sense of clarity.

I'm sure that when I was born my soul was fully aware of everything going on and then arrival in the level of consciousness dominant on the planet, in that area, caused it to shut down and lie dormant to gradually re-awaken in my late twenties.

SELF ORGANISATION:

A week after clearing level 4 (love) as well as feeling my heart more open, my eyes welling with tears whenever I felt gratitude or spoke about my vision — my business began to self-organise. For the first time ever I had partners, staff and functional booking systems and marketing systems that could run without me.

The business began to seem like a living breathing organism that had its own life-force and its own inner order which was beginning to appear without any extra input from me.

I began asking myself — what IS love and how does it impact organisation?

MY best understanding of love is the field of compassionate intelligence that underlies all of existence. An absence of conditions, polarities and emotions and simply a deep feeling of oneness, wellbeing, beauty, connection and good will and well LOVE.

Obviously this is distinct from the "Hollywood" definition of love, which is really a strong emotional infatuation caused by projecting our happiness, completion and need for belonging onto another person.

When we are open to the former (what I would call "heart chakra" love) a natural order simultaneously begins to arise because we are no longer resisting what 'IS'.

From this place of present, loving, gratitude, time and attachment begins to dissolve and systems or natural flows begin to emerge.

If we treat a business as an independent entity then at its heart sit the systems that hold it together. The order we bring to our business is a direct result of how much we love it. Disorder then is a result of emotional or mental blocks that prevent the free flow of love.

TIME IS AN ILLUSION:

Systems thinking is an amazing tool for managing complexity and a useful way of seeing a more accurate representation of reality outside of the limited view that we get through our senses. It gives us the ability to perceive things as systems or flows instead of isolated events.

If I look in my bank account on any given day the amount of money in the bank gives me a snapshot of "how much money do I have right now".

Although it may create an emotional response for me based on whether or not I think that's a lot of money or a small amount, that snapshot is relatively meaningless unless I can place it into some sort of useful context.

In other words I need to find a way to be able to perceive the flow of cash from one month to the next to properly understand what's going on in the business.

Quantum physics encounters the problem of how an electron can show up as a either a particle or as a wave depending on what we look for.

In my personal view this is because at the quantum level (the incredibly small) time collapses and we are seeing pure potentiality.

Since we filter reality based on our perceptions, prejudices and intentions — it is whatever we think it is.

Much like a bunch of sub-atomic particles whizzing through nothingness, we can't SEE our business either.

It's not a fixed point in time or a single event. Rather it's a series of interlocking flows — of relationships, of finances, of products or services delivered, of internal and external communications all of which are (ideally) governed by a central mission, a series of values and numerous project and task based timelines.

It's best understood as a living organism, the health of which is a direct reflection of the alignment of our purpose, vision, values, organisational capabilities, will power, relationships and actions.

This is true whether you happen to be tracking these things or not, although it would seem that what we focus on expands.

This is difficult for our minds, which are so visual to handle which is why businesses use metrics and graphs in an attempt to measure, track and predict the ebbs and flows of the business activity much like a fisherman would keep track of the tides.

Our construct of time confuses us because it causes us to believe that events happen one after another and that the thing that happens first causes the thing that happens next — like a neat little chain of dominos.

From a metaphysical or quantum perspective this isn't what's happening at all.

Another way to understand the laws of cause and effect is that the level of resonance we hold — the frequency we are vibrating at — calls events and outcomes into being.

The day I DECIDED that I was a millionaire and started clearing emotional blocks around having that level of worth is the day that I (on some level) became one.

My ability to hold that resonance (and not the actions I take per se) is going to be what calls that reality into being on a physical level.

This is quite counter to the Newtonian physics take on reality, which is that "a causes b which causes c".

The more meditation, psychedelics, and transcendental practices I've become involved in the more I've come to the conclusion that my ability to attune myself to "ABC" causes "ABC" to manifest.

Any aspect of my life or of my business is resonating at the level of "love" (around 500 on Hawkins scale) will become naturally self organising.

In other words, any area of the business that you don't love will fall into disorganisation or at least will have to be kept in order by effort.

What does this mean?

It means ANY AREA OF BUSINESS OR FINANCE THAT WE HAVE AN EMOTIONAL TRIGGER AROUND (whether consciously or not) WILL CONSTANTLY FALL INTO DISORDER AND DYSFUNCTION.

This doesn't mean you need to be romantically in love with your financial system. It means you need to be able to hold a field of open, grateful, non-reactive consciousness around your finances. Any contraction in you (on a bodily level) around the inflow and outflow of money, around tax, invoicing, profit and loss etc, will cause imbalances and fluctuations in the flow.

This is why I specialise in using kinesiology, NLP based coaching and general tampering with the body's energy field to clear up blocks around business!

WHAT'S THE BIG DEAL ABOUT MONEY?

According to the bible "the love of money is the root of all evil".

I've thought about this often and cannot see this as anything other than an indictment on the energy of attachment itself.

Love in the sense that I mean it refers to an open, connected, transcendent, heart opened — non-attached state of consciousness. From this place there is no such thing as evil, nor does money have any more charge than any other word.

If we are doing business from a place of love, what John Demartini refers to as a place of "fair exchange" it suggests that we are capable of giving, receiving, taking and allowing with equal ease and power.

We are overflowing with abundance and compassion and money can be used as a clean measure for the fair exchange of value. Obviously that's a far cry from where the bulk of society is sitting. A big step towards achieving that is getting clean and clear around what I call:

THE 4 DIRECTIONS OF EXCHANGE:

Giving:

The gift is the essence of value and wealth. Our ability to contribute fully to the world is the cornerstone of our wealth. When we understand it isn't what we get, but what we can give to the world that determines our wealth we are well on the way to breaking the "work hard for money" and the "scarcity" paradigm.

When I meet a person who doesn't have enough money, the first thing I ask them is — "How could you be creating more value in the world?" If we master the art of creating value constantly — we cannot help but increase our worth. It's impossible.

Giving from lack:

There is a shadow behaviour that lurks behind the seemingly innocent surface of the giver. It's the obligated giver or the over giver. Both of these patterns come from a place of low self worth. When we give because we "should" that tells us that guilt is running in the background somewhere like bad spyware on your pc.

Over-Giving:

The over-giver is similar — giving because we feel we aren't enough. These behaviours are like subtle forms of cancer that deplete our energy. Colour the nature of our giving with shades of resentment and prevent us from ever being fully honest with ourselves.

Under-giving:

Stinginess is just as imbalanced (not worse) than over-giving. Every time we contract from a place of "not enough" we affirm to ourselves that we doubt there is enough to go around. In order to not give, to hold back our gift or to dishonestly cover up our contribution communicates deep lack to our unconscious mind.

Taking:

Taking gets a bad rap in our society and yet it is the people who can congruently (and often incongruently) take that become leaders.

To "take" from a place of presence and love is like an eagle swooping down and snatching a salmon from a stream. There is no hesitancy, no self doubt or moral deliberation — the eagle simple swoops and claims what is rightfully his. This assumes two things 1. The thing we are taking is "ecological" and "fair game" and that 2. We are aligned in our action.

Under-active taking:

Due to low self worth, self doubt or social conditioning we don't ask for what we want. We don't want to be seen to stand out of for others to think we are entitled so we curb our needs, desires or ambition. We don't see how being decisive, expressing our desire and prioritising our own needs could possibly serve others. After all — we've been told that its "self-ish".

Overactive/repressed taking:

When we don't believe we are fully worthy or don't think we will get our needs met by other means we employ devious and shadowy forms of "taking". These may include stealing (whether directly or indirectly) as well as cutting down the achievements and success of others.

Receiving:

Receiving is a beautiful, passive, open energy and yet so many of us have been conditioned to believe "we don't deserve it. Healthy receiving is the heart of wealth — it houses the knowledge that we don't have to work to create a result — that the universe is by nature abundant and that we deserve goodness, pleasure and wellbeing 'just' for being ourselves.

Under-active receiving:

People who struggle to receive will often run compulsive giver/nurture/rescuer strategies. Being in constant motion prevents them from the vulnerability require to fully receive. Or they may simply shutdown and block receptivity on an energetic level. This may translate to financial behaviours such as undercharging, not following up on invoices , etc.

Allowing:

Allowing is the ability to "let it be what it is." It is the Zen attitude to life. In business this is essential if we aren't to become micro managers or control freaks. Consciously allowing means we are more able to "manifest" good fortune and turn bad circumstances into good. Really it means we are unattached and nonreactive.

The shadow of allowing is being too permissive. Business is also about defining healthy boundaries and maintaining the integrity of agreements. Sometimes this requires us to be able to "not allow" something i.e. to lay down a strong boundary. People who fear confrontation and disharmony will often err on the side of

"allowing everything". Again this comes down to the fear of not being loved and supported.

WEALTH MINDSET:

The word 'mindset' has long been a non-threatening way to package 'inner-work' for the corporate and mainstream world so it doesn't get scared.

I have numerous clients who describe me as their "mindset coach" to their friends and business colleagues. I figure if throwing chakra clearing, shamanic journeying, Chinese medicine, hypnosis, ritual process and quantum funny business into the category of "mindset" makes it easier to deal with then so be it.

Personal development staples like Awaken the Giant Within and Turning Passions into Profits describe the impact of beliefs and value systems in much greater detail than I'm going to here.

Nevertheless, it's an essential part of this journey so well look into it in as concise a manner as possible. We form all manner of beliefs as we grow up based on the evidence life gives us and the conditioning (in the form of emotional baggage, values, stories and identities) we've accumulated up until that point).

Once a belief is formed we may test it a little but… we tend to consistently find evidence for what we believe. In this way if someone decides (unconsciously) at the age of 5 that "rich people are mean" they will find ongoing evidence, in the form of landlords, bosses and news stories to support this.

Furthermore any attempts to become "rich" will be sabotaged as most people deep down aren't ok with being "mean".

We form hundreds of these sorts of beliefs as we grow. Some are harmless but some will directly prevent us from ever experiencing what we want unless we find a way to change them. How hard it is to change a belief depends on how much that belief is wired into our identity and how much emotion there is reinforcing it.

The most challenging part of changing beliefs is that we don't usually know that we have them. After all they form the windows of our perceptual reality. Seeing your beliefs is like trying to look at your own eyes… difficult – even with a mirror!

What's astonishing to me is how far we can get even with a limiting belief and a bunch of emotional baggage in the way.

During my wealth upgrade sessions I explain that clearing the emotional blocks and redesigning the belief system is like taking the handbrake off a racing car.

If you've already been winning races whilst driving with the handbrake on — imagine what it's going to be like when we take it off!

* I also explain that if your car has no wheels and no engine, we're going to have more work to do that than just "taking the handbrake off".

CHAPTER FOUR EXERCISES:

STEP ONE:
Decide which of the 4 directions of exchange you feel most challenged by:

STEP TWO:
Try these exercises:

Giving:
This week offer 3 people something free of charge — it could be a service or product, it could be a gift of your time, it could be something so as simple as a compliment. Observe the feelings in your body as you make the offer.

Receiving:
Practice receiving gratitude and gifts. If someone thanks you: look them in the eyes and say "you're welcome". If someone offers you a compliment say "thank-you". You're not allowed to dismiss or deflect any incoming abundance or positivity.

Taking:
Find 3 opportunities to claim what you want this week. It could be the eating the last biscuit, it could be making sure you're first in line or simply demanding what you want in any area of your life. Write your demands below!

Allowing:
Where are you being a control freak? In what areas would your life of or business flow more easily if you let go? What can you delegate?

CHAPTER FIVE

RESPECT MY AUTHORITY

"When the voice and the vision on the inside is more profound, and more clear and loud than all opinions on the outside, you've begun to master your life"

– Dr. John Demartini

I remember as a 4 year old, one day when I was off sick from school and my grandmother was taking care of me. The main mistake she made was taking me to the office where she had a cleaning job and leaving me alone in a room by myself.

Once I had grown bored with my toys and comic books I realised there was a phone in the room. Of course I called emergency services and when they asked me "which service do you require" I answered confidently "fire" and hung up.

The parental disciplinary fallout from that experience was fairly severe but it failed to rid me of one conviction I've had my whole life — that authority was in the eye of the beholder and that if I wanted to get anywhere in life I'd have to develop my own inner authority.

As I began writing this book I started to ask myself the question that many authors must: "Who am I to express my opinion? What do I know? Why would anyone give a shit about what I have to say?"

Once we've overcome our fear of not surviving, and our fear of not belonging and started taking action and started organising ourselves — we must lead, and in order to lead — we have to take the risk of expressing ourselves.

The only way to find our voice is to start using it. This can be a tough gig when we've been raised to follow elected leaders and respect authority figures.

I've often wondered what the world would look like if instead of projecting our own inner authority onto "leaders" and then blaming them when they inevitably fail to represent us, we recognised each individual as an authority in their own right.

This sort of talk sometimes seems a bit rich coming from a kid who's had difficulty with authority his whole life.

If you're reading this book it seems likely that you are either already doing something that is a meaningfully driven attempt to express something new or special into the world, or you want to.

There is something in each of us that calls us to be more. It calls us to grow beyond our old limitations and stretch ourselves in the same way that a plant grows towards the sun. It also calls us to express something unique of ourselves into the world. We ARE creators of one kind or another and we are here to evolve — of that much I'm 100% certain. In order to fully honour that call we have to do one thing more than anything else — we have to back ourselves as an authority.

In order for this to be valid and not a total delusion it means we have to be authentic. I'm not an authority on science, or economics or health or even business in the general sense, but... I am an authority on MY perspective, my experience and the particular insights that has provided me.

The same is true for you.

THE DOMINANT PARADIGM:

The current form of capitalism that dominates is a dysfunctional expression of that drive for growth and expansion. Much like a cancer cell, a company or corporation that grows simply for the sake of growing can be incredibly destructive if left unchecked. I wonder if everyone was fully expressed and confident in themselves and their offering, if consumerism in its current form would be quite so necessary?

What if instead of consumption to fill the gaps in our collective soul we consumed only what we needed to, to express our creativity?

I don't believe that growth in and of itself is a bad thing. Nor is the pursuit of financial wealth and abundance. In fact I believe that MOST people would like to experience a richer life than the ones they currently lead and that the underlying cause of that drive (beneath the existential emptiness many people feel) is the natural drive of consciousness wanting to unfold and expand.

Every single person I've ever worked with has something they've wished to express or share with the world and everyone I've ever done Wealth Clearing or a Wealth Upgrade session with has had numerous unconscious emotional blocks and limitations preventing them from fully receiving (or even asking for) what they're worth. This has applied to multi-millionaires just as consistently as broke 20 somethings starting their first business.

Whenever I hear someone say "money isn't everything" or "rich people aren't happy anyways" or something like that I always ask myself — did this person express everything they are, value themselves as a person and THEN decide money wasn't important to them? If so that's awesome.

What I often find is that people have written off financial abundance because they either believe "it's impossible/ too hard" or they perceive it as a destructive pursuit that they associate to corporate greed, pollution and rampant consumerism.

I deeply relate to these concerns and still hold some of them myself although I also feel that these concerns can be used to cover up the low self worth and fear of "not being enough" that riddles the majority of the human race.

Personally I'm committed to using wealth and business growth as a vehicle for shedding any and all resistance I'm holding to fully expressing my creativity and uniqueness to the world. I can't think of a more appropriate vehicle for that than building businesses that efficiently and ecologically help people whilst giving me a channel for my creativity and intelligence.

I also believe that a large part of the reason people have difficulty reconciling business with a spiritual path is because they run an "either/or" view of the world. They carry the (limiting) belief that it has to be a choice. "be good OR be rich". "be spiritual or be business savvy". I've spent the last 15 years reconciling these paths and experimenting with both of them.

I've found that business is a mirror of who I am (just like any other pursuit) and that a large percent of the negativity and unworthiness people feel around business is because they don't really believe they deserve financial abundance.

INNOVATORS GONNA INNOVATE...

The source of all our wealth as a planet is innovation. The guy who buys something, marks it up and sells it on hasn't made anything new. Neither have the vast majority of people slaving away inside faceless corporations, filing little sheets of paper and entering numbers into boxes in spreadsheets.

I love that scene in fight club, at the end where all the credit card buildings blow up and for a brief time I wondered if THAT might be a way I could improve our society.

In the end I decided I'd rather create a new paradigm than try to destroy the old one. Besides, I figure they'd have all those records backed up somewhere anyway.

If we agree we want a different world it's our job to create it. To describe it, paint it, build it, teach it's philosophies, write it's stories and lead all those who are ready to move towards it.

If you're reading this book, regardless of political position (they get a lot less important once you decide to really be a creator) you've probably come to the conclusion that government ISN'T going to solve the problems of the world and lead the way to a new paradigm.

Your job is to find your unique message and share it with as many people as possible. That's basically it. It doesn't matter whether you're a financial advisor or a reiki healer, what matters is, do you express what you have to offer the world? Do you continue to refine it each day, each week each month and is that message REALLY aligned with who you are?

The message of this book is that business CAN be a spiritual journey and in fact if you REALLY want to have a fulfilling life and leave a better world, it HAS to be a spiritual journey.

WHAT MAKES A 'CONSCIOUS' BUSINESS ?

The way I see it there are 2 main rules and a handful of principles that make a "conscious" business different from the run-of-the-mill businesses out there.

Rule #1

The **primary** function of the business is to align the creator with his/her higher purpose and deliver the benefits of that purpose as a contribution to the world in a way that is ecological and harmonious with everyone and everything involved.

Rule #2

The building and running of the business is treated as a journey of personal awakening above and beyond just being a way of earning a living.

The business, its successes and failures and every challenge and success and all relationships experienced through the business are recognised as a mirror of who we are and are actively used as a crucible for transformation.

So in other words the business is a vehicle for us to live our purpose, to serve the world and to wake us up to ourselves (ideally whilst making a profit and having a fun adventure at the same time).

Sound like a big ask?

What else are you going to do with your time and energy? ;)

IT'S ALL ABOUT ALIGNMENT!

In some ways using business as an evolutionary vehicle does make it harder than the boring old peddling products and services for money approach.

In other ways though I've come to experience that my business and the businesses like mine have an added resilience and flexibility that the average business doesn't have.

That's because anyone using business in this conscious way is working with the principle of alignment.

Alignment means that the purpose, vision, values, message, systems, actions, relationships and results of the business are all congruent and harmonious with each other.

If the highest purpose of the business is to raise consciousness of the planet or connect women to their sexuality or create sustainable environmental solutions, then the business engages a higher aspect of everyone working in and with the business. When everything is in alignment — things just flow. It isn't about hard work anymore, it's about harnessing the divine order to deliver something beautiful. When this happens the results can seem magickal.

The "Spiritual Business Plan" process outlined in chapter 7 is a process that will help align and realign every aspect of your business.

CHAPTER FIVE EXERCISES:

NUMBER ONE:
List the top 7 most powerful and rewarding feelings you want to experience as you build your business and live your life:

My Example:
Strength, Creativity, Freedom, Joy, Fulfilment, Clarity, Connection

NUMBER TWO:
List the top 5 values by which you will run your business.

My example:
Connection, Abundance, Honour, Evolution, Results.

CHAPTER SIX

MAGICKAL THINKING

"Reality is what you can get away with"
– Robert Anton Wilson

I was tired of living in a second rate, poorly decorated apartment. I decided to try out the sigil magick process I'd learned a few years earlier and see if I couldn't "magick" myself up a new apartment.

I put on some otherworldly, mystical sounding music, lit some incense and a candle and wrote my intention "new, clean, apartment" on a piece of paper and gradually began crossing out repeated letters and started weaving the remaining ones into a "sigil" — an arcane symbol made from the letters spelling out the intention you want to manifest.

I let my mind relax and a new strange symbol began to form from my repeated doodling until I had something that looked suitably weird and felt powerful.

I then took it out onto my balcony, read some words out that signified my trusting my intentions to the universe and my unconscious mind and unceremoniously burnt the paper — releasing my desire to the world.

I then took a shower, watched some TV and strategically forgot all about it.

One week later, returning from a retreat I'd been on I switched on my phone to got a barrage of messages from the neighbour, a plumber and the landlord. Apparently whilst I was away the water heater had burst, destroying the carpets, the tiles (which I hated) and ruining the paintwork in several rooms. On speaking to the landlord I was informed I'd have to stay somewhere else for a week whilst they re-painted, re-carpeted and re-tiled the whole apartment.

When I finally walked in, the place looked like a completely different apartment. A "new" apartment. Holy shit. Careful what you wish for....

OUTCOME FOCUS:

Perhaps the single most important skill required to be an effective entrepreneur (or creator or manifestor of any kind) is the ability to hold in your mind the outcome you want.

The ability to do this regardless of what current circumstances are telling you and oblivious of the emotions that may arise on the way towards that outcome is a rare and valuable skill.

The ability to set an intention, see it clearly, treat it as real and move towards it with absolute trust — whilst letting go of attachment to it, is in my opinion one of the most useful abilities a person can cultivate.

Steve Jobs was well known for his "reality distortion field" — a sense of conviction so strong that many engineers and technicians found themselves agreeing to produce impossible results by impossible deadlines. They often found themselves inexplicably delivering those results.

MIRROR THEORY:

For all of this to work it depends on the acceptance of Carl Jung's principle that "perception is projection". In other words, anything that happens or anything we see or experience — is a projection of our own consciousness.

This can be a challenging principle to live by and it helps if you know how to clear your issues as they arise (see my free self clearing training online).

This idea rubs a lot of people up the wrong way because they (correctly) interpret it to mean that any emotional response they have to anything is a reflection of who they are.

The power of this idea is — it forces you to take responsibility for things. If you have 3 unhappy clients in a row, it's highly likely that "the world" aka your unconscious mind is trying to give you some feedback.

Every difficulty I've ever come across has been a mirror of some sort of inner incongruence or unconscious block I've been running. When I finally dare to fully face and own those block (whether they be around worth, or integrity or organisation or leadership or any of the other areas that running a business demands of me) it allows me to integrate that aspect of myself, upgrade and move on.

BE > DO > HAVE:

We've looked at how the human mind tends to confuse effects or end results with the actual root cause of the result.

This is partly because of our physiology and our dependency on the senses — hard science is bound by what it can measure and the man in the street tends to trust in what he can see, hear or touch.

It's also partly because we don't understand the nature of time. We bind ourselves with language and labels that become self fulfilling.

The statement "John IS fat" for example creates a binding and permanent reality. It fails to take account of the fact that John is actually an ever changing process. The molecules that make up John today are not the same ones that made up John a decade ago. John was once a small child, he will one day be a corpse — without attempting to freeze John in time and lock him into a static definition we can't really presume to know what John REALLY is.

HAVING;

On the most superficial, obvious level we HAVE results. When most people think about what they want — they go straight to the HAVE.

I want to have rock hard abs, a hot wife or husband, a Ferrari or a house in the south of France.

Not one of these things is a CAUSE. They are all effects. None of them will happen unless certain behaviours turn up in our lives.

DOING;

Most successful people — that is to say people who get the results they want in one or more areas are "action" people. They DO. The best athletes as well as the best entrepreneurs take action often and quickly without over-analysis.

Just doing something will often lead us to an understanding of how to do it better next time. This is the reason I encourage people to try out their ideas by selling them to people – this forces them to take action – to finish the product, to run the workshop, to make the deal. From this place of action come results.

The personal development world and the sporting world are all about "getting things done" . We learn to "take massive action" and we'll get results. Of course this is effective to a point.

Have you ever tried to "take massive action" and found that you didn't get anywhere?

Have you ever encountered some form of sabotage or resistance that stopped you — or at least made it difficult to "do the do"?

BEING;

Being is about aligning with our inner identity. If an action contradicts our perception of who we are it will be difficult to complete or will cause dissonance later on. It's hard to become rich if you deeply believe rich people are arseholes and you want to be a good person. Something will give out somewhere along the line.

In order to have alignment and ease, our BEING must be aligned with our DOING. 90% of the work I do with my clients is on the BEING level. People that come to me who are running a $1M+ per year business have already figured out the DOING part of the equation.

What they need is greater emotional congruence. Deeper alignment with our identity values mean that action becomes effortless and we begin to RESONATE at the level of our desired results.

IDENTITY:

On the level of being — one of the most powerful conceptual structures that we can attach ourselves to is that of an identity. When we are able to design a new identity and let go of an old one e.g.,"I'm not an employee anymore, now I'm a spiritual business owner", this allows us to drop hundreds of beliefs and patterns and literally become a different person. It is when a specific behaviour conflicts with one of our core identities that we really start to have difficulties pursuing a given path. This is why working on ourselves at the BEING level is critical if we want to be capable of behaviours that no-one in our family line has ever done before.

THE FORMULA OF MANIFESTATION:

Another way to look at the way we manifest results into the world is to look at it as a downwards flow of energy through the chakras (this is the principle behind the Spiritual Business Plan in chapter 7). This takes us through 7 steps to create a result, whether that result be a cup of tea or a new house.

1. PURPOSE – connection to a reason why

2. VISION – seeing a clear outcome in mind

3. EXPRESSION – being able to accurately describe the result

4. OPENNESS TO RECEIVING – gratitude and loving self enough to receive

5. TAKING ACTION – doing something

6. EMOTIONAL CONNECTION – linking pleasurable emotions to the result

7. DESERVING THE RESULT – being worthy on a physical level

CLEARING & INCONGRUENCE:

The process of Clearing means strategically letting go of an emotional response to a thought or feeling.

There are many modalities and practices that include elements of clearing emotions. I created a new, upgraded form of Self Clearing which is much faster and more effective than many of the older tools used for clearing emotions (e.g., NLP, EFT, traditional kinesiology etc).

The process can be learned in minutes and free video trainings can be downloaded from both www.danetomas.com and www.clearyourshit.com

If we have any emotional incongruence at any level of the BE/DO/HAVE model or of the Formula of Manifestation model we will have to use effort to PUSH the result into being. This typically means the process is not smooth and effortless which will lead to stress and loss of energy in other areas of life (e.g., health, relationships, etc), and it can also mean that the results we force into being are not 100% aligned with who we are.

The more congruent we are on the BEING level — the easier the DOING part of the equation and the more fun the HAVING part will be.

THE WEALTH UPGRADE SESSION:

In 2013 I began using kinesiology to measure what my unconscious mind thought I was worth financially. To my surprise I was still running a story that I deserved to earn only $60,000 per year — my old salary back when I had a job.

I had noticed that when I was "at risk" of making too much money in a month I would slow down my sales efforts, "forget" to get back to some prospects and generally find ways to slow things down.

Once I moved the blueprint up into the hundreds of thousands (and later into the millions) my income began to increase rapidly. Of course I was already doing the DO part of the equation – the money didn't just come from nowhere. In May 2014 I had my first $60,000 MONTH.

After this experience I designed a "wealth upgrade" session for other people too. I realised that by moving the internal blueprint (also sometimes referred to as "wealth resonance") we raised the person's income ceiling.

This session is ideal not just for people who want to bring in more money but also for people who want to expand their impact in the world. Once we get clean around it — it's not about money anymore — it's about aligning our be — do — have and living a life that's abundant, fulfilling and that makes a contribution to the world.

CHAPTER SIX EXERCISES:

1. CHOOSE ONE SPECIFIC OUTCOME YOU WANT TO CREATE:

2. WHAT DO YOU PERCEIVE COULD STOP YOU?

3. WHAT DO YOU NEED TO KNOW/BELIEVE TO OVERCOME #2?

4. WHAT WILL IT GIVE YOU WHEN YOU HAVE THE RESULT?

5. WRITE A BRIEF DESCRIPTION OF WHAT YOU CAN SEE, HEAR AND FEEL THE DAY AFTER CREATING YOUR DESIRED OUT COME:

PART TWO

THE SPIRITUAL
BUSINESS PLAN

"GOOD THINGS COME TO THOSE WHO
HUSTLE"

– Anais Nin

TO FAIL TO PLAN IS TO PLAN TO FAIL:

So far this book has laid out a philosophical blue-print of the levels of thinking and ways of looking at the world that can be helpful in moving into a more conscious type of business than the one that currently dominates our world.

This section outlines a structure that replaces the old school business plan and gives a fast and very practical structure for designing a business that connects to a higher purpose and then brings that purpose down into the physical world with grounded, practical steps.

The central inspiration for the business plan is aligning the planning sections with the different chakras, which just happens to align exactly with the steps of the formula of materialisation discussed in Chapter 6.

Here are the sections of the Spiritual Business Plan.

Crown Chakra: Purpose
Third Eye Chakra: Vision
Throat Chakra: Message
Heart Chakra: Boundaries, Systems, Avatar
Solar Plexus Chakra: Immediate goals
Sacral Chakra: Team & Community
Base Chakra: Next Actions

Whenever we follow this process it aligns us with the highest and most abstract level of our business and connects us to the "soul" of our business. As we work down through the categories we are able to get very clear on each level of the business, what it looks like, how it works, what the rules are, what our goals are, who we need to help and what we do next.

I have found that most business coaches are strong at one particular level e.g., they love doing vision and purpose but suck at marketing and implementation OR they are very details oriented and cannot connect someone to their highest reason WHY they want to build the business.

The following is a practical guide on how to take yourself through the Spiritual Business Planning process. This is suitable for both a first time business plan (this usually takes a little longer) and an ongoing check-in process for an existing business. It usually takes me about 20 minutes to whizz through this and get clarity on one or more areas of my business.

Crown Chakra: Purpose Statement

This section addresses the high level "why" of the business. This is useful to connect us to inspiration and drive and to "chunk us up" from day-to-day operations as well as energy sucking fears and concerns.

When this part of a business isn't present it will lack vitality and inspiration, this can typically be felt when we deal with the people in the business.

It's typical for the purpose to be stated in high-level abstract terms. A purpose is not usually something that can be easily "ticked off" like a goal and if it is it's a vast, ambitious goal of epic proportions.

The best way to measure whether the purpose is clear is whether it makes you feel inspired or not.

Questions to help:

Why do you want to build this business?
Why does that matter?
How will it contribute to the world?
What problem does it solve?
What opportunity does it create?
What does it give you to move towards that purpose?
Why this business and not a different one?

Example of a purpose statement:

"to raise the consciousness of the planet"
"to supply organic food to the world"
"to revolutionise the education system"
"to connect women to their sexuality"

Third Eye Chakra: The Vision

The vision is by definition a description of how the business will materialise in the physical world. It should clearly describe what the day-to-day operations of the business will look like so that you can picture it in your mind.

Your "perfect day" exercise will feed into this level of the Spiritual Business Plan.

If this level is unclear it's very difficult to know whether the business is on track and what to do next. Clearing at this level can be very useful as often we will block our vision out of fear or unworthiness.

Questions to help you clarify your vision:

Where does it take place?
How big is it?
Who is involved?
What are the day-to-day actions taking place?
What are the flow-on effects of the business?
What are the positive impacts?
What role do you see yourself playing?
What is the main product/service?
How is it delivered?

What are the top 5 emotions you want to feel whilst building this business?

Example of a vision statement:

Tens of thousands of people are joining my online training program from all over the world. Everyday I receive testimonials from people as far as Mexico and Japan telling me how much they are feeling more alive and vital since doing the exercises.

I love logging into the forums and seeing people helping each other with exercise and diet plans — it all looks so professional and works beautifully – I love the green logo and how smooth the interface is.

I also feel very grateful to be able to log in from anywhere in the world and upload new yoga videos and know that I can help ten thousand people by just spending 5 hours a week shooting videos and writing article…"

Throat Chakra: The Message

Your message is a clear, concise explanation of what you wish to share with your target market and what you wish to represent to the world. Whilst the purpose and the vision are inside your mind, the message is what the outside world will receive and how they will perceive the business. Your message also contains your voice and your brand.

** Awareness of your avatar (ideal client) will also feed back into your message

Questions to help you clarify your message:

What do you want to broadcast to the world?
What is the style or "voice" of your business?
What are the 5 core values you want your business to represent?
What is your brand about?
What do you want people to realise about themselves?
What are the platforms on which you will communicate?

Some examples of message:

"Business can be a vehicle for personal awakening"
"You can still have a great body even if you're a busy mum"
"There is an alternative to eating genetically modified food"
"You create your own reality"

Heart Chakra: Boundaries

As the heart chakra is the centre of the chakra system so is it the centre of your business. At this level I currently use 3 categories — all of which align to the ideas of Love and Order outlined in Chapter 4. They are:

Boundaries:

These are the conditions of business you set both for yourself and for the business. One of the signs that a person loves themselves is that they have standards. The boundaries are the standards that preserve the order and integrity of your business so that you can love yourself whilst running it and so that you can serve your particular avatar with love.

Questions to clarify the boundaries:

What are your rules for who you/your business works with?
What are your rules for yourself within the business?
What are your rules around payment terms and invoicing?
What are the ethics of your business?
How will you enforce these boundaries?

Examples of boundaries:

I only work with people who fit my avatar description
I only work 3 days per week.
I refuse to work with any company that is not ecologically
    sustainable
I require payment up front for all products.
All clients need to fill out a 5 page client questionnaire.

Heart Chakra: Systems

Systems regulate the quality and efficiency of everything that happens in your business, saving you both time and energy and taking care of your customers and clients. Systems can include simple step-by-step processes followed by you or your staff (manual systems) and also include processes that are delivered by various automated processes. A system isn't just the software it's the "what you do" with the software to get the same result each time.

Questions to identify needs for systems:

What are all of the tasks that need to take place in the business?

Which of those tasks can be done by someone else/automated?

What are the step-by-step breakdowns for the tasks you will delegate?

Which areas of your business are in disorder?

Examples of systems:

Lead generation system
Lead conversion system
Booking system
Accounting system
Project Management system
Operating Rhythm
Calendar/to do list system

Heart Chakra: Avatar

One of the most useful and misunderstood concepts in modern niche-marketing (i.e., anything that isn't selling to "everyone" like Walmart or Coles) is the idea of having an avatar.

Avatar is the client you LOVE working with and who you will target all of your messaging and marketing and product design towards.

Rather than a relatively broad demographic (e.g., men aged 30 – 40) avatars are a far more focused, far more detailed representation of your ideal clients. In fact a proper avatar manifests as an actual person with a name, hopes, fears and dreams.

You may have one avatar or several depending on your products and services.

Really KNOWING your avatar means you can get your message to the person who REALLY needs you because you know their needs.

Questions to help you clarify your avatar:

Is it a man or a woman?
What is their name?
How old are they?
What do they do for a living?
What is their relationship status?
Do they have kids?
What are their interest and passions?
What specific problems do they currently have?

What specific goals do they have?

What products/services/media do they currently consume?

What keeps them awake at night?

Example of an avatar

Celeste is a 42 year old mother of two who founded her own brand of organic, low allergenic cosmetics after being dissatisfied with what was on the market. She's happily married to Tate, a 45 year old corporate lawyer and has 2 school aged children both under the age of 10.

Celeste is in great shape and takes care of her health and wellbeing. She loves yoga and Pilates and likes quality brands and products, e.g., lule lemon yoga wear, Aesop soaps and drives an Audi.

She loves socialising with her girlfriends and has attended all manner of spiritual and personal development work-shops in the last 10 years. She considers herself "spiritual but mainstream". She likes Taylor Swift.

She loves her life and her family and her main frustration is that her business hasn't quite taken off to the level she would like.

^^ the above is a medium level of detail for an avatar.

Over time we should REALLY get to know this people.

This isn't numbers in a database — this is a real person.

I revisit my Avatars every 3 to 6 months and update them based on the clients I'm working with presently, who I've enjoyed working with, who gets enormous value from my work and who I want to work with next.

Solar Plexus Chakra: Goals

Now we know a lot about the big picture business and who it's targeted at serving. It's time to set some actual timed and measurable outcomes.

With fast moving small businesses (anything under $5m a year) I don't believe it's that important to have goals over 1 year in length.

If you're using your business as a vehicle for personal discovery and if you are doing other personal development work or clearing work you will be changing very quickly and so will your business.

For some people even 1 year is too far in the future. Gone are the days of giant business plans — you should be able to bust this out on one to two sheets of paper.

Rules for goals:

Choose 3 main goals per year or per 90 day period.

Include one financial income or profit goal.

All goals must be measurable, i.e., a number that can be reached or a project that can be ticked off a list.

Examples of goals:

The business will reach a total income of $300,000 by the 31st December 2015.

I will have an automated lead generation system bringing in 50 leads per month by March 30th 2015.

We will deliver our new yoga course to 300 people by 31st December 2015.

I recommend breaking these main goals down into tasks, and setting them up in a project management app such as 'trello' or 'asana' with deadlines and reminders so that you can accurately track your progress.

Sacral Chakra: Team & Community

Inside the business:

Your team can be defined as everyone who helps you get your goals achieved as well as supports you to build your business. This can include employees, contractors, interns and anyone else who can help you get things done.

Questions to clarify team:

What are the tasks I cant do myself?
What are the tasks I would prefer not to do myself?
What are the skills needed to achieve my goals?
Who do I need to assist me?

Examples:
Lawyer, accountant, business mentor, virtual assistant, graphic designer, publicist, events coordinator, financial advisor, social media curator , etc.

Outside the business:

Are you building a client base or are you leading a movement or building a community? These can all be different things. Building a community (or a tribe) is a core part of something that goes beyond the realms of just a 'normal' business.

For those of us who want to change culture it's about fostering a spirit of community and collaboration so our ideas and message can spread.

Questions:

Who is your tribe?
What platforms can you use to develop your community?
Who already has access to the people you want to connect with?
What events or resources could you provide to bring your existing community together more?
How could you enable your existing clients to network, connect and support one another?

Base Chakra: Next Actions

The whole purpose of the Spiritual Business Plan is to connect us to the highest purpose, clarify our vision and message, structure the organism that we want to grow around our idea clients, set our goals and to bring on the support of any key team members we need to make it happen.

None of this matters if we don't take immediate action.

Being able to chunk down into tiny, relevant actions frees us from the overwhelm of being stuck in the abstract world of our grandiose vision. It helps us realise we don't have to save the world — we just have to send an email!

Questions to get clear on next actions:

What are the top three things I need to do to start moving towards my goals?

Pick one. Do it!

Examples of next actions (note: they are small steps)

Write proposal
Email Bob
Call last month's clients and offer workshop

READING LIST:

Throughout this book I have touched on many concepts that go deep with an assumption that the reader either knows about them already or has the acumen to look them up and learn about them if they need to.

Although this book is really influenced by hundreds of different thinkers and authors here are some of the books that will help you understand the central themes and references in this book.

Spiritual

Chakras: Wheels of Life – Anodea Judith
The Power of Now – Eckhart Tolle
Power Versus Force – Dr David Hawkins

Business:

Ready, Fire, Aim – Michael Mastersson
Eat People – Andy Kessler
The personal MBA – Josh Kaufman
The Cashflow Quadrant – Robert Kiyosaki

Systems/Productivity:

Thinking in Systems: A primer – Donella H Meadows
Getting things done fast – David Allen

Money:

The Trick to Money is having Some – Stuart Wilde
The Science of Getting Rich – Wallace D Wattles
Think & Grow Rich – Napoleon Hill
Turning Passions into profit – Christopher Howard
How to Make One Hell of a Profit and Still Get to Heaven
   – John Demartini

Human Behaviour

Tribes – Seth Godin
Influence – Robert Cialdini
Spiral Dynamics - Don Beck & Christopher Cowan
Awaken the Giant Within – Anthony Robbins
The Biology of Belief – Bruce Lipton

ACKNOWLEDGEMENTS

I always like to pretend I'm an American musician collecting a grammy when I write these kind of things. I'd look out into the crowd overflowing with saccharine sincerity and start by thanking God – except when I say "God" I really mean the swirling quantum consciousness of infinite potentiality that permeates all things including myself so I guess I should start by thanking myself!

To Vanessa, I fucking love you, I love the dance of being two comets hurtling through the sky, of being two snakes ever shedding skins and re-meeting each other with new levels of truth, and joy and intensity and sensitivity. I feel so profoundly inspired by your spark, initiated by your honesty and realness and supported by your love and beauty: thank-you for being you, exactly as you are.

To Mum, Dad and Caroline "chops" Newton. Thank-you all for loving me and for being such an incredibly loving and understanding family.

Mum I'm so grateful you encouraged me at every twist and turn from reading my dinosaur books, to bailing me out of jail and I'm so glad you see angels and talk about "energy". You're such a huge part of who I am.

Dad I will forever remember being carried over the moors on your shoulders and being dragged across snowy hilltops on sledges – I had such an awesome childhood because of you and I feel like I'm really only realising what a sense of adventure you taught me. I've always been very inspired by your ingenuity and hard work and the wheelings and dealings I grew up around are what taught me how to "hustle" in the first place.

Caz – I love you. I'm always inspired by watching your journey and I feel like we're getting to know each other on a new level lately. So many beautiful memories of our childhood came through whilst I was writing this. Oh and for the record – I don't want a pickle.

To all the people who've inspired me, challenged me, taught me something mentored me, given me a push or otherwise believed in me:

Jerome Calvar, Brian Parker, Kerry Kershaw, Sharon Pearson, Grant Lenaarts, Alice Hammerle, Chloe Prendergast, Rachel Anastasi, Gulliver Giles, Leela Cosgrove, Shae Matthews, Brad Sims, Mark Robinson, Eben Pagan, Dr John Demartini, Graeme Orr, Uwe Jacobs, and of course Jay Z – THANK-YOU.

To all Spiral Practitioners, Integrated Men, EVERYONE who's done Spiral, Self Clearing, Soul Values, Wealth Clearing and everyone who's ever done some kind of work with me or trusted in me and my ideas and projects – THANK-YOU.

FIND DANE ONLINE:

To book me for talks, say hello, work with me, read my blogs or book in for a Wealth Upgrade Session:

New website: www.danetomas.com

Clearing & Spiral: www.clearyourshit.com and www.thespiralclearingprocess.com

Facebook: www.facebook.com/dragonflymusick (or search Dane Tomas)

Twitter @danetomas

Instagram @dane_on_the_road

YouTube Dane Tomas

DANE TOMAS BIO

Dane Tomas is a thought leader, conscious entrepreneur and all round personal transformation uber nerd.

His interests are: entrepreneurship, creating new and exciting models for changing human behaviour and raising consciousness, standup comedy, rap music, ritual magick and studying tantra and conscious masculinity.

PROCESSES DANE HAS CREATED:

Self Clearing:

The fastest most permanent way to clear your emotional blocks and redesign your life. You can learn it online for free in about 20 minutes.

The Spiral:

The deepest emotional baggage clearing process known to man. Equivalent to about 7 years of personal development in 7 weeks — if you haven't done spiral — you should do spiral. It will make the journey outlined in this book much easier!

Wealth Upgrade Sessions:

On application Dane takes conscious business owners through a process that clears the specific blocks that prevent you from choosing your own level of wealth and worth. Typically this process can take your wealth resonance to 5 times its original level within 90 minutes. Apply via admin@thespiral.com.

Printed in Great Britain
by Amazon

83871958R00068